Workbook

panish
One

Second Edition

Workbook

Spanish One

Second Edition

Sonia Jones
Antonio Ruiz Salvador

Dalhousie University

D. VAN NOSTRAND COMPANY
New York • Cincinnati • Toronto • London • Melbourne

D. Van Nostrand Company Regional Offices:
New York   Cincinnati

D. Van Nostrand Company International Offices:
London   Toronto   Melbourne

Published by D. Van Nostrand Company
135 West 50th Street, New York, NY 10020

10 9 8 7 6 5 4 3 2 1

Preface

The exercises in this Workbook supplement those in SPANISH ONE,
Second Edition and provide mainly written practice. The scope
of the vocabulary and grammar of each chapter in the basic text
has been maintained in the corresponding chapters of the Workbook.

This Workbook may effectively be used in conjunction with the text
for class and homework. It includes Spanish-English and English-
Spanish vocabularies, thus eliminating the need for consulting the
text vocabularies.

The pages are perforated to facilitate the checking of homework.

Preface

Workbook

Spanish
One

Second Edition

Lección 1

A. Los artículos definidos

Give the definite articles of the following nouns:

1. _____ diálogo   5. _____ mujeres   9. _____ días

2. _____ teatros   6. _____ literatura   10. _____ música

3. _____ filosofía   7. _____ poema   11. _____ gatos

4. _____ alma   8. _____ hombre   12. _____ mano

B. Los artículos indefinidos

Give the indefinite articles of the following nouns:

1. _____ poemas   4. _____ diálogos   7. _____ hombres

2. _____ gato   5. _____ alma   8. _____ teatros

3. _____ mujer   6. _____ manos   9. _____ día

C. Los adjetivos

Change according to the model:

Ejemplo: una mujer sincera (hombre)

          un hombre sincero

1. una mujer inteligente (hombre)

   _____

2. un profesor sentimental (profesora)

   _____

3. un hombre canadiense (mujer)

   _____

1

4. unas mujeres hipócritas (hombres)

_____

5. unos profesores sinceros (profesoras)

_____

6. un gato egocéntrico (gata)

_____

7. unos poemas románticos (mujer)

_____

8. una profesora ideal (hombre)

_____

D. Las preguntas

Change the following statements into questions:

1. Ud. es español.

_____

2. Frank es una víctima eterna.

_____

3. Las mujeres alemanas son generosas.

_____

4. Todos los profesores son así.

_____

5. Javier es muy oportunista.

_____

6. Es un alma generosa y buena.

_____

7. Los hombres norteamericanos son imposibles.

_____

8. Las mujeres inglesas son ideales.

_____

E. Los negativos

Make the following statements negative:

1. Frank es español.

_____

2. Ud. es alemán.

_____

3. Yo soy canadiense.

_____

4. El poema de Frank es bueno.

_____

5. Las mujeres norteamericanas son hipócritas.

_____

6. Los hombres ingleses son sinceros.

_____

7. La música española es buena.

_____

8. Los dentistas son oportunistas.

_____

F. Express in Spanish:

1. Good morning, Elvira. How goes it? What is that?

_____

2. It's a poem about the ideal man.

_____

3. Oh really? What's he like?

_____

4. Well, he's intelligent, and sincere...

    _____

5. No! Men aren't sincere -- they're opportunists.

    _____

6. Many men are like that, but not all.

    _____

7. All, all. Spanish men, English men, they're all like that.

    _____

8. And women, what are women like?

    _____

9. Women are the victims, the eternal victims.

    _____

10. That's because they're generous and good.

    _____

11. No, it's because they're not hypocritical and opportunistic.

    _____

Lección 2

A. El presente de indicativo de los verbos regulares

Complete the following:

1. Ud. (pay) _____ 6. tú (drink) _____

2. ellas (drink) _____ 7. él (studies) _____

3. nosotros (eat) _____ 8. yo (pay) _____

4. Uds. (study) _____ 9. ellos (live) _____

5. ella (lives) _____ 10. nosotros (eat) _____

B. El posesivo

Express in Spanish

1. the professor's house _____

2. the cat's meat _____

3. the old man's ham _____

4. the Spanish woman's friends _____

5. Frank's poem _____

6. the German men's books _____

7. Javier's hand _____

8. the American women's house _____

9. the cat's water _____

C. Los números

Answer the following questions using the numbers indicated:

1. ¿Cuántos capítulos hay en el libro? (24)

_____

2. ¿Cuántas lecturas hay en el libro? (15)

_____

3. ¿Cuántos hombres hay en la clase? (21)

_____

4. ¿Cuántas mujeres hay en el teatro? (31)

_____

5. ¿Cuántos profesores hay en la Universidad? (39)

_____

6. ¿Cuántos programas hay en la televisión? (6)

_____

D. Express in Spanish:

1.	12 _____		9.	2 _____
2.	7 _____		10.	11 _____
3.	26 _____		11.	8 _____
4.	19 _____		12.	34 _____
5.	38 _____		13.	6 _____
6.	4 _____		14.	13 _____
7.	17 _____		15.	25 _____
8.	9 _____		16.	3 _____

E. Answer the following questions:

1. ¿Cuántos son cinco y cinco?

_____

2. ¿Cuántos son siete y siete?

   _____

3. ¿Cuántos son seis y seis?

   _____

4. ¿Cuántos son ocho y ocho?

   _____

5. ¿Cuántos son diez y diez?

   _____

6. ¿Cuántos son quince y quince?

   _____

F. Express in Spanish:

1. I study philosophy with Professor Moreno.

   _____

2. He studies history with Mr. Villafranca.

   _____

3. We study music with Miss Encinas.

   _____

4. Do you study literature with Mrs. García?

   _____

5. He lives near us.

   _____

6. We live near them.

   _____

7. Do you live near him?

   _____

8. According to them, she's an important woman.

   _____

9. According to you, artificial color is bad.

   _____

10. According to her, Miss Encinas doesn't drink.

    _____

11. According to him, we live near Mr. Gómez.

    _____

12. Thank you very much, Mrs. Hernández.

    _____

13. You're welcome, Professor Moreno.

    _____

14. He's drinking a lot, isn't he?

    _____

15. Well, they're paying, aren't they?

    _____

Lección 3

A. El presente de indicativo de los verbos irregulares

Complete the following:

1. él (puts) _____   6. nosotros (have) _____

2. yo (do) _____   7. Uds. (make) _____

3. Ud. (are worth) _____   8. tú (put) _____

4. nosotros (make) _____   9. ella (does) _____

5. ellos (have) _____   10. yo (am worth) _____

B. Los modismos con <u>tener</u> y <u>hacer</u>

Express in Spanish:

1. It's very cold now.

    _____

2. I feel hot.

    _____

3. He is afraid of women.

    _____

4. She never pays attention to men.

    _____

5. We are very lucky.

    _____

6. Are you (fam. sing.) thirsty?

    _____

7. They don't feel like talking.

_____

8. I am not successful.

_____

9. Are you (form. sing.) in a big hurry?

_____

10. I am twenty one years old.

_____

C. Las palabras de negación

Make the following statements negative:

1. Siempre tengo mucha sed.

_____

2. Nosotros estudiamos algo.

_____

3. Alguien tiene que pagar.

_____

4. Hablan o con el profesor Moreno o conmigo.

_____

D. Express in Spanish:

1. I am neither hot nor cold.

_____

2. I'm not hungry either.

_____

3. You (fam. sing.) don't understand anything.

_____

4. They're not afraid of anyone.

_____

5. We don't ever drink wine.

_____

E. Los pronombres preposicionales

Express in Spanish:

1. What does he have against me?

_____

2. There is nothing for her.

_____

3. She never eats with him.

_____

4. He always studies with me.

_____

5. It's all for you (fam. sing.).

_____

F. Express in Spanish:

1. He's not hot or anything.

_____

2. We're not sleepy or anything.

_____

3. They're not hungry or anything.

_____

4. Are you afraid, or what?

_____

5. Is he in a hurry, or what?

_____

6. Am I right, or what?

_____

7. Aren't you speaking with anyone any more?

_____

8. Isn't he speaking with me any more?

_____

9. Aren't they speaking with us any more?

_____

10. We never pay attention to Javier's brother.

_____

11. She never pays attention to egocentric men.

_____

Lección 4

A. El presente de indicativo de los verbos irregulares

Complete the following:

1. Ud. (hear) _____   6. ellos (say) _____

2. ellas (go out) _____   7. tú (come) _____

3. tú (say) _____   8. Ud. (go out) _____

4. yo (come) _____   9. nosotros (hear) _____

5. nosotros (go out) _____   10. él (says) _____

B. Los adjetivos posesivos

Express in Spanish, clarifying all third persons:

1. your (form. sing.) car _____

2. his house _____

3. their (m.) daughter _____

4. her poem _____

5. your (form. pl.) cat _____

6. our books _____

7. their (f.) parents _____

8. your (fam. sing.) brother _____

C. Los pronombres posesivos

Express in Spanish, clarifying all third persons:

1. Their car is small, and ours is big.

_____

2. My sister is big, but his is enormous.

   _____

3. Her friends are hypocritical, but mine are sincere.

   _____

4. Are they friends of yours (form. sing.)?

   _____

5. She is a friend of mine.

   _____

6. The meat is theirs (m.).

   _____

7. The books are yours (form. pl.).

   _____

8. The hams are hers.

   _____

9. The houses are his.

   _____

10. The car is yours (form. sing.).

    _____

D. Los comparativos

   Express in Spanish:

   1. We are richer than they are.

      _____

   2. He is smaller than I am.

      _____

   3. I am less generous than he is.

      _____

4. They are younger than you (form. sing.) are.

    _____

5. I am as old as you (fam. sing.) are.

    _____

6. She is not as lucky as we are.

    _____

7. You (form. sing.) don't talk as much as I do.

    _____

8. I eat as fast as he does.

    _____

9. She drinks as much wine as I do.

    _____

10. They have as many books as we do.

    _____

E. Los superlativos

    Express in Spanish:

1. She is the richest woman in the world.

    _____

2. He is the best professor of all.

    _____

3. She is the best neurologist in the hospital.

    _____

4. They are the most famous men in Mexico.

    _____

5. He is the worst professor in the University.

    _____

6. It's the worst wine in the world!

_____

7. It's the best meat in the world!

_____

8. It's the biggest house in the world!

_____

9. It's the smallest car in the world!

_____

10. She is the least popular woman in the University.

_____

Lección 5

A. <u>Ser</u> con los predicados

Express in Spanish:

1. What is he like?

_____

2. He is very cynical.

_____

3. She is my sister.

_____

4. We are good friends.

_____

5. How pretty she is!

_____

6. How egoistic they are!

_____

7. They are what they are.

_____

B. <u>Ser</u> con el artículo indefinido

Express in Spanish:

1. Ramón Moreno is a professor.

_____

2. He is a very good professor.

_____

3. Javier is a Mexican.

   _____

4. He is not a typical Mexican.

   _____

5. Sara's father is a doctor.

   _____

6. He is a famous doctor.

   _____

7. Elvira is a Catholic.

   _____

8. She is not a very devout Catholic.

   _____

9. My brother is a Socialist.

   _____

10. He is a sincere Socialist.

   _____

C. Ser con las preposiciones

   Express in Spanish:

   1. Is the meat for her?

   _____

   2. No, it's for you (fam. sing.).

   _____

   3. Is that your car?

   _____

   4. Yes, it's mine.

   _____

5. Whose house is that?

_____

6. It belongs to her parents.

_____

7. What is their house made of?

_____

8. It's made of cement.

_____

9. Where are you from?

_____

10. I'm from the United States.

_____

D. Ser con las expresiones temporales

Express in Spanish:

1. What time is it?

_____

2. It's a quarter past one.

_____

3. Isn't it one thirty?

_____

4. I say it's twenty-five to three.

_____

E. Ser con los días de la semana y los meses del año

Express in Spanish:

1. What day is it today?

_____

2. Today is Tuesday, and tomorrow is Wednesday.

_____

3. And what is the date today?

_____

4. Today is the first of January.

_____

5. No, it's the 31st of December.

_____

Lección 6

A. Los usos de <u>estar</u>

Express in Spanish:

1. Where are you?

   _____

2. I am with Javier.

   _____

3. How is he?

   _____

4. He's fine, thanks.

   _____

5. I'm sick today and I feel old.

   _____

6. Are you jealous?

   _____

7. No, I'm angry and I'm very busy.

   _____

8. My coffee is cold, it's not hot!

   _____

B. Los usos de <u>ser</u> y <u>estar</u>

Express in Spanish:

1. Are you smarter than your brother?

   _____

2. I´m ready now.

   _____

3. His parents are very rich.

   _____

4. The meat is delicious.

   _____

5. Is the apple unripe?

   _____

6. Her car is green.

   _____

7. My mother is very pretty.

   _____

8. She looks pretty today.

   _____

9. My father is young.

   _____

10. He looks young now.

    _____

C. Los adjetivos demostrativos

   Express in Spanish:

   1. That (over there) woman is a doctor.

      _____

   2. She lives in that (nearby) house.

      _____

   3. This coffee is mine.

      _____

4. That (nearby) coffee is theirs.

_____

5. Those (over there) boys live here.

_____

6. These books are yours (fam. sing.).

_____

7. Those (nearby) books are ours.

_____

8. Those (over there) secretaries are friends of his.

_____

9. They live in these houses.

_____

10. They work in that (over there) hospital.

_____

D. Los pronombres demostrativos

Express in Spanish:

1. This car is hers, and that one (over there) is his.

_____

2. Those (nearby) books are ours, and these are yours (form. pl.).

_____

3. Those women(over there) are doctors, and these are professors.

_____

4. That (nearby) apple is green, but this one is red.

_____

E. Los colores

Express in Spanish:

1. fifteen gray cats

   _____

2. twenty-one yellow apples

   _____

3. five orange houses

   _____

4. ten black books

   _____

Lección 7

A. El presente de indicativo de los verbos irregulares

Complete the following:

1. Ud. (see) _____   6. él (runs away) _____

2. ellas (believe) _____   7. tú (see) _____

3. nosotros (run away) _____   8. yo (give) _____

4. Uds. (give) _____   9. ellos (go) _____

5. ella (goes) _____   10. nosotros (believe) _____

B. Los pronombres personales como complementos

Express in Spanish:

1. Are you coming to see us tomorrow?

    _____

2. Yes, and I'm going to give you (fam. sing.) a lesson.

    _____

3. Are you going to talk to me about love?

    _____

4. No, I'm going to show you my poems.

    _____

C. <u>Gustar</u>

Express in Spanish:

1. Do you (fam. sing.) like the idea?

    _____

2. No, I don't like it at all.

_____

3. Do you like generous women?

_____

4. Yes, I like them very much.

_____

5. Do you (fam. sing.) like to dance?

_____

6. No, I don't like it at all.

_____

7. Do we like wine?

_____

8. Yes, we like it a lot.

_____

9. Do you (fam. sing.) like sentimental poems?

_____

10. No, I don't like them at all.

_____

D. El pronombre relativo <u>que</u>

Express in Spanish:

1. Those (nearby) are houses which are worth a lot.

_____

2. Do you (fam. sing.) like the girl who lives in that one (over there)? _____

_____

3. These are the books that belong to Frank.

_____

4. Javier and Pepe are the boys who play the guitar.

_____

5. This is the poem that I like so much.

_____

E. La preposición a

Express in Spanish:

1. I'm not going to dance with you.

_____

2. Aren't you (fam. sing.) coming to visit me?

_____

3. We're learning to play the guitar.

_____

4. He always invites me to dinner.

_____

F. Complete the following dialogue in Spanish using the sentences indicated below. Notice that the English sentences are not in the
right order.

Yes? Do you think he's going to invite me to the movies?

Oh, Frank, why don't we go tomorrow?

I'm going to Javier's house. He's going to teach me to speak German.

Yes, of course, but if he's going out with me tonight, I have to
wear a new dress.

Then I'm going home right now.

No, I don´t understand that, and I don´t believe you, either.

You´re jealous of everyone! 　　·

Frank:　¡Maribel!　¿Adónde vas?

Maribel: _____

_____

Frank:　¡Qué historia!　Tiene ganas de estar contigo, nada más.

Maribel: _____

_____

Frank:　Probablemente.　¿Por qué no?

Maribel: _____

_____

Frank:　Pero, ¿no vas a estudiar el alemán con Javier?

Maribel: _____

_____

Frank:　¡Maribel!　¿Estás loca?　¡Tenemos una cita esta noche!

Maribel: _____

_____

Frank:　¿No comprendes que Javier es un Don Juan?

Maribel: _____

_____

Lección 8

A. El presente de indicativo de los verbos con cambios radicales

Complete the following:

1. Ud. (think) _____
2. ellas (begin) _____
3. yo (close) _____
4. él (defends) _____
5. tú (understand) _____
6. ellos (lie) _____
7. nosotros (want) _____
8. Uds. (warn) _____
9. ella (loses) _____
10. Uds. (want) _____
11. ella (understands) _____
12. tú (lose) _____
13. ellos (close) _____
14. nosotros (think) _____
15. él (warns) _____
16. yo (begin) _____
17. ellas (defend) _____
18. Ud. (lie) _____

B. Los pronombres personales como complementos

Rewrite the following statements changing all nouns to pronouns.

Clarify all third persons with a prepositional phrase:

Ejemplo: Frank le vende los libros a Elvira.

Él se los vende a ella.

1. Javier les manda los chocolates a sus padres.

_____

2. Sara le escribe una carta a su madre.

_____

3. Elvira y Sara le mandan un jamón al Sr. Moreno.

    _____

4. La profesora les da los libros a los estudiantes.

    _____

5. Los muchachos les escriben unas cartas a sus amigas.

    _____

C. Answer the following questions according to the example:

    Ejemplo: ¿Vas a mandarle los libros a tu madre?

               No, no quiero mandárselos.

1. ¿Vas a escribirle una carta a Elvira?

    _____

2. ¿Van Uds. a darles las manzanas a los niños?

    _____

3. ¿Vas a mandarme la guitarra?

    _____

4. ¿Van Uds. a venderle el vestido a Sara?

    _____

5. ¿Vas a decirme la verdad?

    _____

6. ¿Van Uds. a darles el café a las señoras?

    _____

D. Saber y conocer

    Express in Spanish:

1. Do you (fam. sing.) know Mrs. Encinas?

    _____

2. We don't know how to play the piano.

_____

3. Do they know where we live?

_____

4. No, but I know their house.

_____

E. El infinitivo después de las preposiciones

Express in Spanish:

1. I don't feel like dying.

_____

2. I'm tired of living with you (fam. sing.).

_____

3. He drinks a lot in order not to be too sad.

_____

4. Afterwards he'll probably invite you to have dinner.

_____

5. Aren't you (fam. sing.) coming to visit me tomorrow?

_____

F. Complete the following dialogue in Spanish using the sentences indicated below. Notice that the English sentences are not necessarily
   in the proper order.

Why do you lie, my child? You love Javier, a boy who knows nothing
   about anything.

No, you don't love me at all. You think I'm older than your
   grandfather.

Well, if you close your eyes, I'm a veritable Adonis!

31

Because you're worth ten times more than he is. You think he's
   very attractive, don't you?

You defend that idiot? Now I'm beginning to lose my patience.

Elvira: Pero ¡yo lo quiero mucho a Ud., Sr. Moreno!

Sr. Moreno: _____

            _____

Elvira: ¡Si Ud. es muy joven!

Sr. Moreno: _____

            _____

Elvira: Pero, ¿por qué?

Sr. Moreno: _____

            _____

Elvira: Bueno, no es feo...

Sr. Moreno: _____

            _____

Lección 9

A. El presente de indicativo de los verbos irregulares y de los verbos
   con cambios radicales

Complete the following:

1. Ud. (die) _____
2. tú (show) _____
3. yo (count) _____
4. el libro (costs) _____
5. nosotros (find) _____
6. ellas (fall) _____
7. yo (remember) _____
8. Uds. (can) _____
9. nosotros (sleep) _____
10. ella (dreams) _____
11. tú (move) _____
12. yo (bring) _____
13. ellos (return) _____
14. él (dies) _____
15. nosotros (show) _____

16. nosotros (fall) _____
17. ella (finds) _____
18. Uds. (move) _____
19. yo (return) _____
20. ellos (show) _____
21. nosotros (die) _____
22. Ud. (sleep) _____
23. tú (bring) _____
24. las cosas (cost) _____
25. él (counts) _____
26. yo (remember) _____
27. Uds. (dream) _____
28. tú (can) _____
29. yo (find) _____
30. ella (falls) _____

B. El mandato directo con <u>Ud.</u> y <u>Uds.</u>

Express in Spanish, first in the formal singular, then in the formal plural:

1. Shut the door.

   _____

   _____

2. Open the window.

   _____

   _____

3. Come back at two thirty.

   _____

   _____

4. Don't leave now.

   _____

   _____

5. Don't come tomorrow.

   _____

   _____

6. Don't move your eyes.

   _____

   _____

7. Don't begin again.

   _____

   _____

34

C. Los verbos con el complemento indirecto

Express in Spanish:

1. He still has many years left.

   _____

2. Don't your children matter to you at all?

   _____

3. I don't have time to be with them.

   _____

4. What do you (fam. sing.) think of her new book?

   _____

5. I like it very much.

   _____

D. Lo y lo que

Express in Spanish:

1. The sad part is that they don't know her.

   _____

2. Women always do what they want.

   _____

3. Don't you know what's the matter with us?

   _____

4. What scares me is that he loves me.

   _____

E. Complete the following dialogue in Spanish using the sentences indicated below. Notice that the English sentences are not in the
   right order.

   Show me your hands, please. They're trembling a little, aren't they?

Come here, Mr. Moreno, and let me examine you. All right, what's
the matter?

Then don't drink so much, and don't smoke, either. Believe me,
those excesses are very bad for the body.

Doesn't your health matter to you at all? Don't go to taverns so
much! I'm counting on you!

Irving: _____

_____

Ramón: Pues me duelen la cabeza y los ojos.

Irving: _____

_____

Ramón: Es que bebo y fumo mucho.

Irving: _____

_____

Ramón: Pero son muy buenos para el alma.

Irving: _____

_____

Ramón: ¡No me ponga en una situación intolerable! ¡No puedo vivir
sin vino!

Lección 10

A. El presente de indicativo de los verbos con cambios radicales

Complete the following:

1. yo (ask for) _____   5. nosotros (go on) _____

2. Uds. (serve) _____   6. ellos (repeat) _____

3. él (goes on) _____   7. tú (ask for) _____

4. nosotros (repeat) _____   8. yo (serve) _____

B. El mandato directo con <u>tú</u>

Express in Spanish, using the familiar singular:

1. Open the door.

   _____

2. Shut the window.

   _____

3. Come back at four o'clock.

   _____

4. Don't move your hands.

   _____

5. Don't begin again.

   _____

6. Give the books to her. Don't give them to me.

   _____

7. Show the letter to me. Don't show it to them.

   _____

8. Ask him for the lemonade. Don't ask me for it.

_____

9. Send the dresses to them. Don't send them to him.

_____

10. Repeat the numbers to them. Don't repeat them to him.

_____

C. Pedir, preguntar y lo como complemento verbal

Express in Spanish:

1. Ask (form. sing.) her if she wants to come.

_____

2. Don't ask (fam. sing.) your parents for money.

_____

3. Ask (fam. sing.) them where they live.

_____

4. Don't ask (form. pl.) me why I do it.

_____

5. If you (form. sing.) don't want to ask him for his car, then

   tell me. _____

_____

D. La posición de los complementos directo e indirecto

Express in Spanish placing the object pronouns first after the

infinitive, and then before the conjugated verb:

Ejemplo: I don't want to give it to him.

          No quiero dárselo.

          No se lo quiero dar.

1. I'm not going to ask him twice.

   _____

   _____

2. He wants to send it to us.

   _____

   _____

3. We don't want to bring it to her.

   _____

   _____

E. Que con el mandato directo

    Express in Spanish:

    1. Come (fam. sing.) here, I want to talk to you.

       _____

    2. Don't talk (fam. sing.) to me that way, I'm your father.

       _____

    3. Do (fam. sing.) what I tell you, it's already late.

       _____

F. Complete the following dialogue in Spanish using the sentences in-
    dicated below. Notice that the English sentences are not in the
    right order.

    Well, he has a beard and long hair. Shall I go on, or is that
       enough?

    We don't need any money. I think it serves no purpose at all!

    Nonsense! That's why there are wars, because people want to have
    so many things!

My friends and I are going to improve the world. We prefer to be

   poor.

No, you don´t know him. Why do you ask me?

Rosa: ¿Quién es Salvador?   ¿Lo conozco yo?

Sara: _____

   _____

Rosa: Dime quién es Salvador, por favor.

Sara: _____

   _____

Rosa: Bueno, no me pidas dinero porque no te lo voy a dar.

Sara: _____

   _____

Rosa: ¿Ah, no?   ¿Quién te paga la comida, eh?

Sara: _____

   _____

Rosa: Mira, Sara, lo más importante es tener un diploma.

Sara: _____

   _____

Lección 11

A. El presente de subjuntivo: los verbos regulares y los verbos con
    cambios ortográficos

    Escriba el presente de subjuntivo de los verbos siguientes:

    1. ellas (poner) _____   7. yo (pegar) _____

    2. yo (oír) _____   8. ellos (hacer) _____

    3. Ud. (decir) _____   9. tú (empezar) _____

    4. nosotros (buscar) _____   10. yo (seguir) _____

    5. ella (venir) _____   11. Ud. (venir) _____

    6. tú (tener) _____   12. nosotros (salir) _____

B. El presente de subjuntivo: los verbos irregulares y los verbos con
    cambios radicales

    Escriba el presente de subjuntivo de los verbos siguientes:

    1. dar (yo) _____   7. querer (nosotros) _____

    2. ser (ella) _____   8. mostrar (tú) _____

    3. ir (nosotros) _____   9. volver (ellos) _____

    4. saber (Uds.) _____   10. mentir (nosotros) _____

    5. estar (tú) _____   11. pedir (ella) _____

    6. cerrar (él) _____   12. dormir (yo) _____

C. El subjuntivo en los mandatos implícitos

    Exprese en español:

    1. I suggest that you (fam. sing.) come with me.

        _____

2. He prefers that we serve the coffee now.

_____

3. We insist that she tell us the truth.

_____

4. They want me to give them the car.

_____

5. I want to go to the movies tonight.

_____

6. We ask you (form. sing.) to do it right now.

_____

7. Tell (fam. sing.) your aunt to prepare the dinner.

_____

8. Write (form. pl.) to them not to come.

_____

9. Tell (form. sing.) them I'm sick.

_____

10. I beg you (form. pl.) to show me the letter.

_____

D. Los verbos que requieren o el subjuntivo o el infinitivo

Exprese las frases siguientes en español, empleando primero el

subjuntivo y después el infinitivo, según el modelo:

Ejemplo: I advise you (fam. sing.) to write it.

Te aconsejo que lo escribas.

Te aconsejo escribirlo.

1. They don't permit me to go out with you.

   _____

   _____

2. I order you (fam. sing.) to give me a kiss.

   _____

   _____

3. You (form. sing.) can't force me to do it.

   _____

   _____

E. El subjuntivo en los mandatos indirectos y en los mandatos de la
   primera persona del plural

   Exprese en español:

   1. Let's not argue any more.

   _____

   2. Make dinner, then.

   _____

   3. No, let's go to the movies.

   _____

   4. I'm tired. Let's read a book.

   _____

F. Complete el diálogo siguiente en español, empleando las frases indicadas. Las frases inglesas no están necesariamente en orden.

   Well I don't permit you to order me to go out with you.

   Do it yourself, I say.

   Are you crazy? What do you want me to tell her?

I prefer that you prepare dinner for me.

Maribel, I´m asking you please to leave me in peace.

Maribel: Escríbele a tu tía que no venga a visitarte.

Javier: _____

_____

Maribel: Dile que busque otro muchacho para este fin de semana.

Javier: _____

_____

Maribel: Y yo te mando que me lleves al cine.

Javier: _____

_____

Maribel: De acuerdo, no discutamos más. Hagamos las paces,

¿quieres?

Javier: _____

_____

Maribel: Hagámosla juntos.

Javier: _____

_____

Maribel: ¡Que te la haga tu tía!

Lección 12

A. El subjuntivo con los verbos de emoción

Exprese en español:

1. I'm sorry that you (fam. sing.) are sick.

   _____

2. I hope that you will come with me.

   _____

3. It surprises me that you (form. sing.) want to write a book.

   _____

4. It's a pity that he doesn't understand you.

   _____

5. Does it bother her that we will arrive late?

   _____

6. He is afraid that I will hit him.

   _____

7. I'm glad that you know who he is.

   _____

8. Here's hoping she'll take me to the movies!

   _____

B. El verbo deber

Exprese en español:

1. He owes me one hundred pesos.

   _____

2. You should let me pay once in a while.

_____

3. They must think we're very stupid.

_____

4. She ought to be less egocentric.

_____

5. I shouldn't talk so much.

_____

6. He must do it right now.

_____

C. Pero y sino

Exprese en español:

1. She's not ugly. She's pretty.

_____

2. We're not perverse. We're human.

_____

3. They're not talking about you, but about me.

_____

4. He's not only strong, but attractive too.

_____

D. El superlativo absoluto

Exprese en español:

1. Your (form. sing.) cat is hopelessly fat.

_____

2. The Villafrancas are extremely rich.

_____

3. Her house is incredibly small.

_____   _____

4. His sister is extraordinarily pretty.

_____

5. They seem blissfully happy.

_____

6. "Super-irresponsible" is an unbelievably long word.

_____

E. Las exclamaciones

Exprese en español:

1. What a woman!

_____

2. What eyes!

_____

3. How well she plays the guitar!

_____

4. What long hair she has!

_____

5. How incredibly foolish you are!

_____

F. Complete el diálogo siguiente en español, empleando las frases indicadas. Las frases inglesas no están necesariamente en orden.

I hope I live so many years!

Hi, Frank. I'm glad that you come to see me.

I'm afraid you're crazy. I never go out with Maribel.

It's a shame that you have to think that. You must be sick. Do

you have a fever?

Does it bother you very much to tell me why you're so angry?

Frank: Hola, Javier. ¿Qué haces?

Javier: _____

_____

Frank: ¿Ah, sí? ¿No te sorprende que yo te hable?

Javier: _____

_____

Frank: Porque sales con mi novia.

Javier: _____

_____

Frank: ¿Por qué mientes, Javier? No me gusta nada que me mientas.

Javier: _____

_____

Frank: Estoy muy bien, gracias. Espero que un día sepas que eres

un muchacho cruelísimo.

Javier: _____

_____

Lección 13

A. El pretérito de los verbos regulares y de los verbos con cambios ortográficos

Escriba el pretérito de los verbos siguientes:

1. nosotros (spoke) _____ 11. ellos (came back) _____

2. Uds. (ate) _____ 12. yo (touched) _____

3. él (lived) _____ 13. nosotros (thought) _____

4. tú (were born) _____ 14. Ud. (found) _____

5. yo (paid) _____ 15. ellas (saw) _____

6. ellas (spent) _____ 16. yo (explained) _____

7. Ud. (wrote) _____ 17. tú (closed) _____

8. nosotros (lost) _____ 18. él (drank) _____

9. yo (wept) _____ 19. yo (began) _____

10. ellos (left) _____ 20. nosotros (remembered) _____

B. Los usos del pretérito

Exprese en español:

1. Did you (fam. sing.) go to class yesterday?

   _____

2. No, I went to the movies.

   _____

3. Did you (form. pl.) give her the notes?

   _____

4. No, we didn't give her anything.

_____

5. Why didn't they offer me (some) coffee?

_____

6. They didn't see you (form. sing.).

_____

7. Did she lose the money?

_____

8. No, she didn't lose it. She spent it.

_____

9. Did Javier go out with your (fam. sing.) girl friend?

_____

10. Yes, he took her to a restaurant.

_____

11. Did he pay for the meal?

_____

12. No. They washed the dishes afterwards.

_____

13. They didn't enjoy themselves very much, did they?

_____

C. El subjuntivo después de las expresiones de duda

Cambie las frases según el ejemplo:

Ejemplo: Tú crees que voy a hacerlo. (dudo que)

Dudo que tú creas que voy a hacerlo.

1. Ella no viene aquí. (más vale que)

_____

2. ¿Uds. no quieren ir? (es posible que)

_____

3. Va a hacerlo mañana. (no dudo que)

_____

4. Ellos son muy cínicos. (no estoy seguro que)

_____

5. No está en casa. (parece mentira que)

_____   _____

D. El subjuntivo después de las expresiones de negación

Exprese en español:

1. He denies that he knows it.

_____

2. It´s not true that he denies it.

_____

3. I don´t deny that he says it.

_____

4. It´s true that he goes out with her.

_____

E. Complete el diálogo siguiente en español, empleando las frases indicadas. Las frases inglesas no están necesariamente en orden:

   On the contrary! We argued a lot, and she accused me of being
       abrupt with her friends.
   But I don´t want my daughter´s hormones to get the best of me
       (conquer me).
   I am sad because I doubt that Sara can understand me.

51

I don't deny that she's right. But when I see her go out with those
hairy adolescents, I feel like crying.

No, not yesterday, but last week. We went to a restaurant, and
then I took her to the movies.

Elena: ¿Por qué estás triste, Rosa?

Rosa: _____

_____

Elena: ¿Qué pasó? ¿No cenaron Uds. juntas anoche?

Rosa: _____

_____

Elena: Estoy segura que lo pasaron Uds. muy bien.

Rosa: _____

_____

Elena: ¿Es posible que Sara tenga razón?

Rosa: _____

_____

Elena: Bueno, así son los jóvenes. A esa edad están dominados por
las hormonas.

Rosa: _____

_____

Lección 14

A. El pretérito de los verbos con cambios radicales

Complete lo siguiente:

1. Uds. (asked for) _____   12. ellos (preferred) _____

2. él (warned) _____   13. yo (served) _____

3. tú (felt) _____   14. Ud. (lied) _____

4. yo (preferred) _____   15. nosotros (asked for) _____

5. ellas (prevented) _____   16. ella (dried) _____

6. Ud. (repeated) _____   17. yo (warned) _____

7. nosotros (slept) _____   18. él (slept) _____

8. yo (went on) _____   19. tú (prevented) _____

9. ellos (died) _____   20. Uds. (felt) _____

10. nosotros (lied) _____   21. yo (repeated) _____

11. Uds. (served) _____   22. ellas (went on) _____

B. El imperfecto de los verbos irregulares

Complete lo siguiente:

1. tú (used to be) _____   4. Ud. (were seeing) _____

2. él (was going) _____   5. ellos (used to go) _____

3. nosotros (were) _____   6. yo (used to see) _____

C. Los usos del imperfecto

Exprese en español:

1. He used to take them (fem.) to the movies.

    _____

2. He would always invite them to dinner.

    _____

3. Did they like him?

    _____

4. No. His friends were very strange.

    _____

5. Did you used to go to class with him?

    _____

6. Yes. I saw him every day.

    _____

7. What was he like?

    _____

8. Well, he always seemed to be a little sad.

    _____

9. Did he smoke and drink a lot?

    _____

10. No, but he was afraid of everything. His father was very cruel.

    _____

    _____

D. El pretérito y el imperfecto

Exprese en español:

1. What was your (fam. sing.) husband doing when you came back?

    _____

2. When I opened the door, he was writing a letter.

_____

3. I noticed that his hands were shaking a bit.

_____

4. I asked him why he always drank so much coffee.

_____

5. He told me that he was always sleepy, because he was tired of
   living with me.

_____

_____

6. Did you prepare him some more coffee?

_____

7. Of course not! Do you want me to kill him?

_____

8. Did you argue with him?

_____

9. No, but I looked at the letter. It was for his secretary, who
   lives in Cuernavaca.

_____

_____

E   Complete el diálogo siguiente, empleando las frases indicadas.
    Las frases inglesas no están necesariamente en orden.

    Because my wife always criticized them.
    She liked them because she was (a) good person and she was very
        intelligent.
    Yes, please find her, Inspector. I loved her with all my (the) soul.

Why do you say "she was"? Our daughter didn't die, you know.

I don't know, she never used to bring them home.

And I was right! They were all from very bad families.

Inspector: Pero ¿quiénes eran sus amigos, señora?

Rosa: _____

            _____

Inspector: ¿Ah, no? ¿Por qué?

Irving: _____

            _____

Rosa: _____

            _____

Inspector: ¿Por qué le gustaban estos amigos?

Irving: _____

            _____

Rosa: _____

            _____

Inspector: Bueno, voy a hacer todo lo posible para encontrarla.

Rosa: _____

            _____

Lección 15

A. El pretérito de los verbos irregulares

Escriba la forma apropiada del pretérito:

1. saber (él) _____   6. traer (yo) _____

2. poner (nosotros) _____   7. poder (Ud.) _____

3. conocer (Uds.) _____   8. decir (nosotros) _____

4. querer (tú) _____   9. hacer (ellos) _____

5. tener (ella) _____   10. venir (tú) _____

B. El pretérito y el imperfecto

Exprese en español:

1. Yesterday I got a letter from a friend I had in Casablanca.

   _____

   _____

2. He wanted to eat, but she refused to prepare the dinner.

   _____

   _____

3. I met Javier because he used to know my sister.

   _____

   _____

4. We didn't know that they were here; we found out this morning.

   _____

   _____

C. Los números ordinales

Exprese en español:

1. June 1st _____

2. Lesson Eight _____

3. the third month _____

4. the fourth woman _____

5. the first time _____

6. Alphonse the thirteenth _____

7. the second day _____

8. the fifth year _____

9. in the first place _____

D. El gerundio de los verbos regulares e irregulares

Escriba lo siguiente en español:

1. nosotros (are speaking) _____

2. él (is eating) _____

3. Uds. (are living) _____

4. yo (am repeating) _____

5. ellas (are dying) _____

6. tú (are lying) _____

7. Ud. (are going) _____

8. nosotros (are falling) _____

9. ella (is hearing) _____

10. yo (am coming) _____

E. Los usos del gerundio

Exprese en español:

1. What are you (fam. sing.) doing?

_____

2. I'm writing a letter.

_____

3. What were you doing when I arrived?

_____

4. I was listening to the radio. Why?

_____

5. Whom are the children talking with?

_____

6. They're reading a book. Why are you asking me so many things?

_____

_____

7. Were you sleeping this morning when I left?

_____

8. No, I was dreaming about the ideal man.

_____

9. Why weren't you preparing me some (un) coffee?

_____

10. For God's sake, Guillermo! You're driving me crazy!

_____

F. Complete el diálogo siguiente en español. Las frases inglesas no están necesariamente en orden.

I wanted to go but I couldn't, because I was reading and studying.

Hi, Maribel! I thought you were playing the guitar now.

I can't. I didn't bring (any) money.

I was eating when you arrived, and now I don't have anything left.

   I'm very sorry.

Yes, I'm still living (I go on living) there.

Maribel: ¡Hola, Frank! ¿Qué estás haciendo solo aquí?

Frank: _____

          _____

Maribel: No, esta mañana no pude. ¿Por qué no fuiste al concierto

          ayer?

Frank: _____

          _____

Maribel: ¡Pobre Frank! ¿Todavía vives en casa de aquella vieja

          tan cínica y tan melancólica?

Frank: _____

          _____

Maribel: Oye, ¿tienes algo de comer?

Frank: _____

          _____

Maribel: Llévame a comer entonces, ¡anda!

Frank: _____

          _____

Lección 16

A. Los verbos reflexivos comparados con verbos no reflexivos

Exprese en español:

1. He is washing himself.

   _____

2. He is washing her.

   _____

3. I am looking at myself.

   _____

4. I am looking at you (fam. sing.).

   _____

5. She is waking up.

   _____

6. She is waking her up.

   _____

7. They are going to bed.

   _____

8. They are putting him to bed.

   _____

B. Los reflexivos con sentido diferente

Exprese en español:

1. They raised their hands.

   _____

2. They got up early.

_____

3. He asked me the time.

_____

4. I wonder why?

_____

5. He amused me a lot.

_____

6. I always have a good time.

_____

7. A priest married him.

_____

8. He got married in May.

_____

9. He made dinner.

_____

10. She became a doctor.

_____

C. Los verbos que siempre son reflexivos

Exprese en español:

1. They didn't realize that she was here.

_____

2. She always complained about the professors.

_____

3. You (fam. sing.) never remember to bring the books.

_____

4. Well, you (fam. sing.) don´t realize that I´m very busy.

_____

D. El reflexivo recíproco

Exprese en español:

1. They used to love each other then.

_____

2. We used to look into each other´s eyes. (We used to look at each other in the eyes.)

_____

3. They saw each other every week.

_____

4. We hated each other when we (first) met (each other).

_____

5. They never used to write to each other.

_____

E. Complete el diálogo siguiente en español. Las frases inglesas no están necesariamente en orden.

Be quiet, Elena. I know you´re laughing at me.

Then get up and take a hot shower!

What a question! How do you think I´m going to go to sleep when you wake me up every ten minutes?

Please, Elena, don´t start with that. I feel very tired now and I want to sleep.

Well, I didn´t realize anything. Look, maybe tomorrow after I get washed.

Elena: Oye Guillermo, ¿ya te estás durmiendo?

Guillermo: _____

           _____

Elena: Estoy muriéndome de frío.

Guillermo: _____

           _____

Elena: Guillermo, ¿por qué no te arrimas un poco a mí?

Guillermo: _____

           _____

Elena: Yo tenía ganas de hablar contigo.

Guillermo: _____

           _____

Elena: Pero estás tan atractivo ahora mismo.

Guillermo: _____

           _____

Lección 17

A. El participio pasado

Escriba el participio pasado de los verbos siguientes:

1. traer _____   7. ver _____

2. volver _____   8. poder _____

3. romper _____   9. hacer _____

4. morir _____   10. decir _____

5. escribir _____   11. abrir _____

6. cubrir _____   12. poner _____

B. El participio pasado como adjetivo

Exprese en español:

1. We were lost in the enormous hospital.

   _____

2. There are no restaurants open today.

   _____

3. The chocolates are covered with ants.

   _____

4. Do you (fam. sing.) like chocolate-covered ants?

   _____

C. El perfecto de indicativo

Complete lo siguiente:

1. él (has seen)

2. yo (have covered) _____

3. Uds. (have come back) _____

4. nosotros (have broken) _____

5. ella (has put) _____

6. tú (have opened) _____

7. Ud. (have made) _____

8. ellos (have died) _____

9. yo (have said) _____

10. ellas (have written) _____

D. El perfecto de indicativo

Exprese en español:

1. He has already written it.

    _____

2. I have put them under the tree.

    _____

3. We have never been here before.

    _____

4. They have always told the truth.

    _____

5. It has been a fantastic day.

    _____

E. Los pronombres, adjetivos y adverbios indefinidos

Exprese en español:

1. Some have finished, but others are still studying.

    _____

2. Is somebody going to call the police?

_____

3. Have you (fam. sing.) seen any ants yet?

_____

4. No, there are no ants here.

_____

5. Are you (form. pl.) writing to some of your friends?

_____

6. No, we're not writing to any (of them).

_____

7. Anyone can speak Spanish.

_____

8. He falls in love with any woman who passes by.

_____

9. He works more than anyone!

_____

10. Of course, because he has less talent than anyone.

_____

F. Complete el diálogo siguiente en español. Las frases inglesas no
están necesariamente en orden.

Of course! I haven't slept all night, and I haven't eaten anything
decent in three days.

We're going to eat something.

I'm telling you, there's nobody anywhere!

No, I haven't seen any yet.

Well, we're lost, but we have to get there some day.

I don't intend to do anything.

Sara: Oye, Salvador, ¿viene algún coche?

Salvador: _____

_____

Sara: Creí que venía alguien. ¿No has oído nada?

Salvador: _____

_____

Sara: ¿Tienes sueño, o qué?

Salvador: _____

_____

Sara: ¿Qué vas a hacer entonces?

Salvador: _____

_____

Sara: Pero no sabemos dónde estamos.

Salvador: _____

_____

Sara: Y ¿qué vamos a hacer ahora?

Salvador: _____

_____

68

Lección 18

A. El futuro de indicativo de los verbos irregulares

Complete lo siguiente:

1. ellas (will come) _____   6. ellos (will say) _____

2. tú (will have) _____   7. ella (will be worth) _____

3. Uds. (will put) _____   8. Uds. (will leave) _____

4. él (will want) _____   9. tú (will know) _____

5. nosotros (will do) _____   10. él (will be able) _____

B. Los usos del futuro

Exprese en español:

1. She will never love me.

   _____

2. Will you (form. pl.) come to see me tomorrow?

   _____

3. He will never get married.

   _____

4. They will be happy some day.

   _____

C. El subjuntivo después de las expresiones conjuntivas

Exprese en español:

1. I'll come, provided that he lets me.

   _____

2. He's going to prepare dinner so that I can go out.

   _____

3. What are you going to do if (in case) she talks to him?

   _____

4. I'll leave without her realizing it.

   _____

5. Give (fam. sing.) it to me before they arrive.

   _____

6. We'll eat now, unless you (fam. sing.) are not hungry.

   _____

7. Even though they say they will do it, I don't believe them.

   _____

8. I gave it to him, in spite of the fact that he didn't want it.

   _____

D. Los diminutivos

   Exprese en español:

   1. Poor little thing! _____

   2. Come here, little boy. _____

   3. Eat, little daughter. _____

E. El subjuntivo después de las expresiones conjuntivas que se refieren al futuro

   Exprese en español:

   1. Will you (fam sing.) call me when you get back?

      _____

   2. He called me when he got back.

      _____

70

3. I'll do it as soon as I can.

_____

4. I did it as soon as I could.

_____

5. They will stay here until she comes.

_____

6. They stayed here until she came.

_____

7. He always comes in while I'm washing the dishes.

_____

8. He came in while I was washing the dishes.

_____

9. You'll (fam. sing.) understand her better after you have
   children.

_____

10. I understood her better after I had children.

_____

Complete el diálogo siguiente en español: Las frases inglesas no
están necesariamente en orden.

And when I get married, can we go on being friends?

Well, I love you very much, in spite of the fact that you don't
    believe me.

I'll remember you until you forget me.

Yes of course, provided that you invite me. When do you plan to die?

It seems to me that you're exaggerating a bit.

I'll never get married, unless I meet an ideal man.

71

Ramón: ¿Qué tengo que hacer para que me quieras?

Elvira: _____

_____

Ramón: ¿Vendrás a llorarme en mi lecho de muerte?

Elvira: _____

_____

Ramón: El día de tu boda.

Elvira: _____

_____

Ramón: Te casarás con un tonto perdido.

Elvira: _____

_____

Ramón: No, niñita. Yo nunca hablo con las niñas que se estropean
la vida.

Elvira: _____

_____

Ramón: Mientras estés lavando los platos, acuérdate de tu viejo
amigo.

Elvira: _____

_____

Lección 19

A. El potencial de indicativo de los verbos irregulares

Complete lo siguiente:

1. ellas (would come) _____   6. él (would be able) _____

2. tú (would have) _____   7. yo (would say) _____

3. Uds. (would put) _____   8. ellos (would be worth) _____

4. él (would want) _____   9. Uds. (would leave) _____

5. nosotros (would do) _____   10. tú (would know) _____

B. Los usos del potencial

Exprese en español:

1. I wouldn't say that!

   _____

2. Couldn't you do it for me?

   _____

3. He promised her that he wouldn't drink any more.

   _____

4. I told him I would tell him the truth.

   _____

C. El futuro y el potencial perfectos

Escriba la forma apropiada del futuro perfecto:

1. volver (nosotros) _____

2. morir (yo) _____

3. romper (Uds.) _____

4. abrir (tú) _____

5. escribir (ella) _____

Escriba la forma apropiada del condicional perfecto:

6. hacer (ellos) _____

7. decir (Ud.) _____

8. poner (nosotros) _____

9. ver (yo) _____

10. ir (tú) _____

D. Los usos del futuro y del potencial perfectos

Exprese en español:

1. He will have arrived by tomorrow.

_____

2. If she comes at noon, I will have already left.

_____

3. They would have gone crazy.

_____

4. In that case, I wouldn't have married you.

_____

E. Los usos de para

Exprese en español:

1. They won't have time to feel lonely.

_____

2. She's keeping the chocolates for her children.

_____

3. When do you (form. sing.) leave for Mexico?

_____

4. I have to be at the University by one o'clock.

_____

5. For such a rich man, he's very generous.

_____

6. Nowadays there are other alternatives for men.

_____

7. Do you have plans for the vacation?

_____

8. You're doing everything possible to make me furious.

_____

9. Does one have to get married to be happy?

_____

10. He's very wise for such a young boy.

_____

F. Complete el diálogo siguiente en español. Las frases inglesas no están necesariamente en orden.

Nonsense! I wouldn't say that.

That's why I married you, because since you were very poor my mother thought you'd never become a doctor.

That's why I have a headache. You always talk to me slowly and emphatically, but meanwhile I'm dying of anxiety.

Couldn't you shout a little less? I have a headache.

Yes, but my own daughter told me that she'd have children one day with that Salvador.

Irving: Hoy día los jóvenes no hacen nada para dar gusto a sus padres.

Rosa: _____

_____

Irving: ¿Ah? Y, de otra manera, ¿no te habrías casado conmigo?

Rosa: _____

_____

Irving: Te casaste conmigo para hacer rabiar a tu madre.

Rosa: _____

_____

Irving: No estoy gritando. Te estoy hablando en voz muy baja.

Rosa: _____

_____

Irving: Rosa, me prometiste anoche que no te morirías de angustia.

Rosa: _____

_____

Irving: Pues con alguien tendrá que tenerlos.

Lección 20

A. El pluscuamperfecto

Complete lo siguiente:

1. él (had seen) _____

2. **yo** (had covered) _____

3. Uds. (had come back) _____

4. nosotros (had broken) _____

5. ella (had put) _____

6. tú (had opened) _____

7. Ud. (had made) _____

8. ellos (had died) _____

9. yo (had said) _____

10. ellas (had written) _____

B. Los usos del pluscuamperfecto

Exprese en español:

1. We still hadn't seen it.

    _____

2. I had already written to them.

    _____

3. We had never been there before.

    _____

4. Had you (form. pl.) done it already?

    _____

5. She hadn't gone to bed yet.

_____

C. Los usos de <u>por</u>

Exprese en español:

1. I think she lives around here.

_____

2. They're going to leave tomorrow morning.

_____

3. We ate at four in the afternoon.

_____

4. I want to talk for the three of us.

_____

5. Thanks for your (form. sing.) letter.

_____

6. You (fam. sing.) married me out of sheer spite!

_____

7. She went for them at a quarter to nine.

_____

D. Verbos y modismos con <u>por</u>; complementos preposicionales; <u>mismo</u>

Exprese en español:

1. Unfortunately he had already left.

_____

2. Apparently he was in a hurry.

_____

3. We should keep quiet for the time being.

_____

4. That's why he worries about her.

_____

5. In general she takes him for an idiot.

_____

6. At last they asked after me.

_____

7. He does it for himself, not for them.

_____

8. She always talks about herself.

_____

9. They think about themselves too much.

_____

10. I made it myself.

_____

E. Complete el diálogo siguiente en español. Las frases inglesas no
   están necesariamente en orden.

   One moment, Frank. Why don't you wait until tomorrow afternoon or
       night?

   Yes, but when I called her, she hadn't gotten up from her nap yet.

   For God's sake Frank, calm down! I went for her at three-thirty,
       but she had already gone out.

   Apparently she has gone with Javier to take a stroll around the
       park.

Frank: Elvira, ¿hablaste con Maribel? ¿Te has preguntado por mí?

Elvira: _____

_____

Frank: Pero, ¿No la llamaste por teléfono antes?

Elvira: _____

_____

Frank: ¿Dónde está entonces?

Elvira: _____

_____

Frank: Bueno, ¡vámonos al parque nosotros también!

Elvira: _____

_____

Frank: ¡Es que no puedo! ¡Odio a Javier con toda el alma!

Lección 21

A. El perfecto de subjuntivo

Escriba las formas apropiadas del perfecto de subjuntivo:

1. nosotros (ver) _____

2. Uds. (volver) _____

3. yo (escribir) _____

4. ella (ir) _____

5. tú (decir) _____

6. ellos (romper) _____

7. Ud. (cerrar) _____

8. nosotros (abrir) _____

9. él (ser) _____

10. yo (querer) _____

B. Los usos del perfecto de subjuntivo

Cambie las frases según el ejemplo:

Ejemplo: No ha hablado con ellos. (siento que)

Siento que no haya hablado con ellos.

1. Hemos llegado temprano. (se alegra de que)

_____

2. Se han levantado a las siete. (espero que)

_____

3. No ha olvidado nada. (ojalá que)

_____

81

4. No has podido decirme la verdad. (lástima que)

_____

5. No hemos estudiado esta noche. (no me gusta que)

_____

6. Han estado enfermos. (sentimos que)

_____

7. No me has comprendido bien. (temo que)

_____

C. El subjuntivo después de antecedentes indefinidos

Exprese en español:

1. I'm looking for a man who is really independent.

_____

2. We need someone who knows how to do it.

_____

3. I know someone who knows how to do it.

_____

4. They will do what they can.

_____

D. La voz pasiva

Exprese en español:

1. The books were written by some friends of mine.

_____

2. He will be invited by the President.

_____

3. We were elected members of the Academy.

_____

4. Spanish is spoken here.

   _____

5. It is believed that young men don't know what they're doing.

   _____

6. Many cases are seen where it isn't true.

   _____

7. The doors are opened at eleven in the morning.

   _____

8. They have been invited to stay until tomorrow.

   _____

9. I have been told that he's not coming.

   _____

10. The programs were mentioned by my uncle.

    _____

E. Complete el diálogo siguiente. Las frases inglesas no están

   necesariamente en orden.

   It always bothers me to have old formulas repeated to me.

   I've never felt better in all my life.

   Why do you lie, child? I don't like you to lie to me.

   It's a shame that you think that you have to tell me new and original

   things.

   I'll bet you're surprised that I haven't died a long time ago.

   Elvira: ¡Hola, profesor Moreno! ¿Cómo se encuentra Ud. hoy?

   Ramón: _____

            _____

Elvira: ¡Vaya! Me alegro de que se sienta tan bien.

Ramón: _____

_____

Elvira: Al contrario, temo que Ud. nos sobreviva a todos.

Ramón: _____

_____

Elvira: Pues siento que me haya tomado tan en serio.

Ramón: _____

_____

Elvira: Pero es muy difícil contarle cosas nuevas.

Ramón: _____

_____

Elvira: Es que temo que Ud. ya haya oído todo mil veces.

Lección 22

A. El imperfecto de subjuntivo

Escriba la forma -ra del imperfecto de subjuntivo:

1. tú (pedir) _____   9. él (querer) _____

2. él (poder) _____   10. tú (oír) _____

3. Uds. (poner) _____ 11. Ud. (ver) _____

4. yo (saber) _____   12. yo (morir) _____

5. ellos (venir) _____ 13. ellas (seguir) _____

6. nosotros (dormir) _____ 14. nosotros (traer) _____

7. Uds. (estar) _____ 15. tú (caer) _____

8. ella (dar) _____   16. ella (sentir) _____

B. El pluscuamperfecto de subjuntivo

Escriba el pluscuamperfecto de subjuntivo

1. abrir (ellos) _____

2. escribir (Ud.) _____

3. volver (yo) _____

4. decir (ella) _____

5. poner (nosotros) _____

6. ver (él) _____

C. La correlación de tiempos

Cambie las frases según el verbo indicado:

1. Sugiero que te calles.

   Sugerí _____

2. Dígale que no lo haga.

   Le dije _____

3. Le pedirá que no venga.

   Le pidió _____

4. Siento que estés enfermo.

   Sentí _____

5. Quiero que me lo digas.

   Quisiera _____

6. Nos gusta que nos diga la verdad.

   Nos gustaría _____

7. Dudo que lo hayan escrito.

   Dudaba _____

8. Me alegro de que lo hayas hecho.

   Me alegré _____

9. Quiero que tú me lo des.

   Quería _____

10. Siento que todavía no haya vuelto.

    Sentí _____

D. El subjuntivo en las condiciones contrarias a la realidad

Exprese en español:

1. I would tell (it to) him if I knew (it).

   _____

2. I would have told (it to) him if I had known (it).

_____

3. If I invited him, he would come.

_____

4. If I had invited him, he would have come.

_____

5. Would you (fam. sing.) lie if you had to do it?

_____

6. Would you (fam. sing.) have lied if you had had to do it?

_____

E. Exprese en español:

1. They are looking at us as though we were crazy.

_____

2. He treats us as though we were hopeless fools.

_____

3. Don't speak (fam. sing.) to me as if I weren't capable of understanding.

_____

_____

F. Complete el diálogo siguiente. Las frases inglesas no están necesariamente en orden.

Such an idea never would have occurred to me in a hundred years.

It's not true that I'm afraid of being alone.

If I told him that, he wouldn't pay any attention to me anyway.

I wouldn't say so (much)! He's a typical husband.

When you're my age, Elvira, maybe you'll understand me better.

Elvira: ¿Por qué no le dices a papá que deje de salir con su
secretaria?

Elena: _____

_____

Elvira: Entonces, ¿por qué no te divorcias de él?

Elena: _____

_____

Elvira: ¿Por qué no? ¡Te trata como si fueras una criada!

Elena: _____

_____

Elvira: Tú tienes miedo de quedarte sola. Por eso no te divorcias
de él.

Elena: _____

_____

Elvira: Entonces, ¿qué temes?

Elena: _____

_____

Lección 23

A. El subjuntivo con expresiones impersonales

Cambie según el verbo indicado:

1. Es dudoso que llegue a tiempo.

   Era _____

2. Es de esperar que nos lo digan.

   Era _____

3. Es necesario que lo hagamos.

   Será _____

4. Es una pena que no puedas ir.

   Fue _____

5. Es probable que tenga que hacerlo.

   Era _____

6. Parece mentira que sepas leer español.

   Parecía _____

7. No es posible que venga aquí.

   No era _____

8. Es importante que vayamos a verlo.

   Era _____

9. No es justo que se lo hayas dicho.

   No era _____

10. No hay duda de que la quiere mucho.

    No había _____

B. El subjuntivo con expresiones impersonales

Exprese en español:

1. Here's hoping we will meet him when he comes.

   _____

2. It is necessary to do it right away.

   _____

3. It is important for us to tell him the truth.

   _____

4. It is true that she wanted to see me.

   _____

5. Is it possible that they are here now?

   _____

6. It was a shame they couldn't go.

   _____

7. Was it necessary for him to shout so much?

   _____

8. It was important for them to stay here.

   _____

9. There was no doubt that he hated his wife.

   _____

10. It was true that she didn't love him either.

   _____

11. Was it necessary for her to kill him?

   _____

12. It was doubtful that she could have succeeded.

   _____

13. It's not true that she went to the doctor this morning.

_____

C. El gerundio

Exprese en español:

1. By studying, one learns a lot.

_____

2. By living with you (fam. sing.), I understand you better.

_____

3. As I was going home, I saw Javier.

_____

4. While he was with Maribel, he remembered everything.

_____

5. Since they drank the same wine, both got sick.

_____

D. Complete el diálogo siguiente. Las frases inglesas no están

necesariamente en orden.

It's true that it's a little old. It will be necessary for me to

fix it up before I set sail.

I'm not going to tell you anything, because it's very doubtful that

you are capable of understanding.

It's evident that you don't know anything about anything. All I

need are the stars and the moon and the sun.

Yes? Well, it's impossible for you to know everyone.

It doesn't matter that it's small.

Javier: ¿Tú piensas dar la vuelta al mundo en un barco tan

pequeñito?

Frank: _____

_____

Javier: Pero es muy viejo, hombre.

Frank: _____

_____

Javier: ¿Qué piensas hacer en caso de que te pierdas?

Frank: _____

_____

Javier: ¡No me vas a decir que sabes de navegación celeste!

Frank: _____

_____

Javier: Yo soy muy conocedor de la naturaleza humana.

Frank: _____

_____

Lección 24

A. <u>Quien</u>

Exprese en español:

1. The woman he went out with last night is a friend of mine.

   _____

2. The girls you (form. sing.) saw yesterday work in the hospital.

   _____

3. The man they work for lives near me.

   _____

4. There are the little boys I talked to you (fam. sing.) about.

   _____

B. <u>¿De quién?</u> y <u>cuyo</u>

Exprese en español:

1. Whose books are these?

   _____

2. Whose dishes are they washing?

   _____

3. There is the woman whose son is a doctor.

   _____

C. ¿Qué? y ¿cuál?

Exprese en español:

1. What is eternity?

   _____

2. What is a businessman?

   _____

3. What is his problem?

   _____

4. What are their desires?

   _____

D. El cual

Exprese en español:

1. This is the little girl I'm so worried about.

   _____

2. It's a book I couldn't live without.

   _____

3. Javier's friends, (the ones) who live in Cuernavaca, are
   arriving soon.

   _____

   _____

E. Lo cual y lo que

Exprese en español:

1. He prepares the dinner, which is no small thing.

   _____

2. She works too, which helps me a lot.

   _____

F. El que y ello

Exprese en español:

1. He who says little is wise.

_____

2. Those who know most talk least.

_____

3. I didn´t realize it.

_____

4. He is not very convinced about it.

_____

5. I don´t want to think about it.

_____

G. Sujetos y complementos pronominales amplificados por sustantivos

Exprese en español:

1. We men are the eternal victims.

_____

2. We women have to work more.

_____

3. They spoke with us students.

_____

4. He gave it to you boys.

_____

H. Complete el diálogo siguiente. Las frases inglesas no están
    necesariamente en orden.

    Look, I spend hours talking to men with whom I have nothing in
        common and in whom I have no interest at all.

Come on, you know very well that the life of a businessman like me
   is ridiculous.

I don't help anyone, don't you see? We businessmen don't serve any
   purpose at all (don't serve for anything).

But what I do is not important. I spend the entire day doing abstract calculations for which they pay me a salary.

Irving: ¿Por qué tanto pesimismo esta mañana, Guillermo?

Guillermo: _____

           _____

Irving: No te sigo. ¿Cómo que ridícula?

Guillermo: _____

           _____

Irving: Pero por lo menos haces algo importante.

Guillermo: _____

           _____

Irving: Pues ayudas a la gente, lo cual no es poca cosa.

Guillermo: _____

           _____

Irving: Bueno, todo es relativo. ¡No te preocupes tanto!

Vocabularios

adj.	adjective	m.	masculine
adv.	adverb	pl.	plural
demonst.	demonstrative	poss.	possessive
dir. obj.	direct object	prep.	preposition
f.	feminine	prep. pron.	prepositional pronoun
fam.	familiar	pron.	pronoun
form.	formal	rel.	relative
ind. obj.	indirect object	sing.	singular
inf.	infinitive	subj.	subject

ESPAÑOL-INGLÉS

This vocabulary is intended to be complete for all Spanish words in the Workbook.

a to, at
abrir to open
absoluto absolute
aclarar to clarify
aconsejar to advise
acordarse (ue) de to remember
acuerdo (m.) agreement; de acuerdo O.K.
adjetivo adjective
¿adónde? where? (with verb of motion)
adverbio (m.) adverb
agua (f.) water
¿ah? oh?; ¿ah, sí? oh, really?
ahora now; ahora mismo right now
al (a el) to the; al contrario on the contrary
alegrarse (de) to be glad
alemán German
algo something
alguien someone, somebody
algún, alguno some, any
alma (f.) soul
amigo (m.) friend
amplificar to amplify
¡anda! come on!
angustia (f.) anxiety
anoche last night

antes before
año (m.) year; tener...años to be...years old
apellido (m.) last name
apropiado appropriate
apunte (m.) note
aquel that
aquí here
arrimarse to snuggle up
artículo (m.) article
así thus; so; that way; like that
atractivo attractive
aunque even though
ayer yesterday
ayudar to help

bajo low; short
barco (m.) boat
bastar to be enough
beber to drink
bien well
boda (f.) wedding
buen(o) good; all right; buenos días good morning
buscar to look for

cabeza (f.) head
caer to fall
café (m.) coffee
caliente hot
callarse to keep quiet,
  to shut up
cambiar to change
cambio (m.) change
canadiense Canadian
capítulo (m.) chapter
carta (f.) letter
casa (f.) house; estar
  en casa to be at home;
  ir a casa to go home
casarse (con) to get married
caso (m.) case; en caso de
  que in case, if
causa: a causa de because of
celeste celestial
cenar to dine
cerrar (ie) to close, to
  shut
cinco five
cine (m.) movies
cínico cynical
cita (f.) date, appointment
clase (f.) class, classroom
coche (m.) car
color (m.) color
comer to eat
comida (f.) food, meal
como as, since
¿cómo? how, what?; ¿cómo
  es...? what is...like?
comparado compared
comparativo comparative
complemento (m.) object
completar to complete
comprender to understand
con with; con tal que provided that
concierto (m.) concert
condición (f.) condition
conjuntivo conjunctive
conmigo with me
conocedor (m.) connoisseur
conocer to know, to be acquainted with; to meet
  (for the first time)
contar (ue) to tell, to re-
  late
contigo (fam. sing.) with
  you

contra against
contrario contrary; al contrario on the contrary
correlación (f.) sequence,
  correlation
cosa (f.) thing; no es poca
  cosa it's no small thing
creer to believe, to think
criado (m.) servant
cruel cruel
¿cuál? what?, which?; el
  cual which, who, whom;
  los cuales which, who,
  whom, the ones; lo cual
  which
¿cuándo? when?; ¿para
  cuándo? (by) when? (deadline)
¿cuánto(s)? how much?, how
  many?
cuatro four
cubrir to cover
cuyo whose

chocolate (m.) chocolate

dar to give; dar la vuelta
  al mundo to go around the
  world; dar gusto to please
de of; de acuerdo O.K.; de
  repente suddenly
deber to owe, ought, must
decir to say, to tell
dejar to let; dejar de to
  stop
definido definite
del (de el) of the
demostrativo demonstrative
demasiado too much
dentista (m. & f.) dentist
después (de) after, afterwards
día (m.) day; buenos días
  good morning
diálogo dialogue
dieciséis sixteen
diferente different
difícil difficult
diminutivo diminutive
dinero (m.) money
diploma (m.) diploma

directo direct
discutir to argue
divorciarse (de) to divorce
doler (ue) to hurt; me duele
  la (cabeza) I have a (head)-
  ache
dominado dominated
¿dónde? where?
dormir (ue, u) to sleep;
  dormirse to go to sleep
dos two
duda (f.) doubt
dudar to doubt
dudoso doubtful

e and (before i and hi)
edad (f.) age
egocéntrico egocentric
ejemplo (m.) example
el the
él (subj. pron.) he; (prep.
  pron.) him
el que he who, the one who
ella (subj. pron.) she;
  (prep. pron.) her
ellas (subj. pron.) they;
  (prep. pron.) them
ello it
ellos (subj. pron.) they;
  (prep. pron.) them
empezar (ie) to begin
emplear to use
emoción (f.) emotion
en in
encontrar (ue) to find;
  encontrarse to feel
enfermo sick
entender (ie) to understand
entonces then
es he, she, it is; es que
  it's just that
escoger to choose
escribir to write
eso that
español Spanish
esperar to hope, to wait;
  es de esperar it is to be
  hoped
esposa (f.) wife
esta this; esta noche tonight
estar to be
este this
estropear to spoil, ruin

estudiante (m. & f.) student
estudiar to study
estúpido stupid
eterno eternal
exclamación (f.) exclamation
explicar to explain
expresar to express
expresión temporal (f.) expression of time

fantástico fantastic
favor: por favor please
fecha (f.) date
feo ugly
filosofía (f.) philosophy
fin (m.) end; por fin at
  last
frase (f.) sentence
frío (m.) cold
fumar to smoke
futuro (m.) future

ganas: tener ganas de to
  feel like
gato (m.) cat
generoso generous
gente (f.) people
gerundio (m.) gerund, present participle
gracias thank you
gritar to shout
guardar to keep
guitarra (f.) guitar
gustar to like, to be pleas-
  ing to
gusto (m.) pleasure; dar
  gusto to please

haber (auxiliary verb) to
  have
hablar to speak, to talk
hacer to do, to make; hacer
  las paces to make up
hay there is, there are
hielo (m.) ice
hipócrita hypocritical
historia (f.) story; history
hola hi
hombre (m.) man
hoy today; hoy día nowadays
humano human

ideal ideal
imperfecto imperfect
impersonal impersonal
implícito implicit, implied
importancia (f.) importance
importante important
importar to matter
imposible impossible
indefinido indefinite
indicado indicated
indicativo indicative
indirecto indirect
infinitivo infinitive
inglés English
inteligente intelligent
intolerable intolerable
ir (se) to go
irregular irregular

jamón (m.) ham
joven young; (m.) young man;
  jóvenes (m. pl.) young
  people
juntos together
justo fair, just

la the
lástima (que) it's a
  shame (that), it's
  a pity (that)
lavar to wash
le (ind. obj. pron./form.
  sing.) (to) you, (to) him,
  (to) her, (to) it
lectura (f.) prose passage
lecho (m.) bed (archaic)
leer to read
les (ind. obj. pron./form.
  pl.) (to) you, (to) them
levantar to lift, to raise;
  levantarse to get up
libro (m.) book
limonada (f.) lemonade
lindo pretty
literatura (f.) literature
lo (dir. obj. pron.) you,
  him, it; lo cual which;
  lo que what, that which,
  which; lo triste the sad
  thing
loco crazy
los (pl.) the

llamar to call
llegar to arrive
llevar to take, to carry
llorar to weep, to cry

madre (f.) mother
malo bad
mandar to send
mandato (m.) command
manera (f.) way; de otra
  manera otherwise
mano (f.) hand
manzana (f.) apple
mañana tomorrow; mañana
  por la mañana tomorrow
  morning; esta mañana
  this morning
más more; más vale (que)
  it is better (that)
medio half; media hora
  half an hour
mejor better
melancólico melancholy
menos less; por lo menos
  at least
mentir (ie, i) to lie
mentira (f.) lie; parece
  mentira it seems incredible
mes (m.) month
mí (prep. pron.) me
mi(s) my
miedo: tener miedo (de)
  to be afraid (of)
mientras (que) while;
  mientras tanto meanwhile
mil a thousand
mirar to look (at)
mismo same; itself; ahora
  mismo right now; el libro
  mismo the book itself; el
  mismo libro the same book
modelo (m.) model
moderno modern
modismo (m.) idiom
morir(se)(ue, u) to die
mostrar (ue) to show
muchacha (f.) girl
muchacho (m.) boy
mucho much, a lot
muerte (f.) death
mujer (f.) woman; wife
mundo (m.) world; dar la

vuelta al mundo to go
around the world
música (f.) music
muy very

nada nothing, not...any-
thing; at all
naturaleza (f.) nature
navegación (f.) navigation
necesario necessary
negación (f.) negation
negativo negative
ninguna parte nowhere, not...
anywhere
niño (m.) child, little boy
no no, not
noche (f.) night; esta noche
tonight
norteamericano American
nos (dir. or ind. obj. pron.)
us
nosotros (subj. pron.) we
novia (f.) girlfriend, fiancée
nueve nine
nuevo new
número (m.) number

o or; either
ocupado busy
ocho eight
odiar to hate
oír to hear
ojalá here's hoping
ojo (m.) eye
olvidar to forget
oportunista opportunistic
orden (m.) order
ordinal ordinal
ortográfico orthographic,
spelling
otro another; de otra manera
otherwise
oye hey, listen

paciencia (f.) patience
padres (m. pl.) parents
pagar to pay
palabra (f.) word
papá Dad
para for; para siempre for-

ever; para que so that
parecer to seem
parque (m.) park
parte; ninguna parte (f.)
nowhere, not...anywhere
participio (m.) participle
pasado past
pasar to happen; pasarlo
bien to have a good time
pasivo passive
paz (f.) peace; hacer las
paces to make up
pedir (i, i) to ask (for)
pegar to hit
pena (f.) shame, pity
pensar (ie) to think; pensar
inf. to intend
pequeño little, small
perder (ie) to lose; perderse
to get lost
perfecto perfect, present perfect
permitir to permit
pero but
persona (f.) person
personal personal
pesimismo (m.) pessimism
plato (m.) dish
plural plural
pluscuamperfecto (m.) past
perfect
pobre poor
poco(s) few, little; no es
poca cosa it's no small
thing
poder (ue) to be able; no
puedo I can't
poema (m.) poem
poner to put
por for; by; por eso that's
why; por favor please; por
fin at last; por lo menos
at least
¿por qué? why?
porque because
posesivo possessive
posible possible
posición (f.) position
potencial conditional
predicado (m.) predicate
preferir (ie, i) to prefer
pregunta (f.) question
preguntar to ask; preguntar

por to ask after
preocuparse to worry
preparar to prepare
preposición (f.) preposition
preposicional prepositional
presente present
pretérito preterit
primero first
probable probable
probablemente probably
problema (m.) problem
profesor (m.) professor
programa (m.) program
prometer to promise
pronombre (m.) pronoun
pronominal pronoun (adj.)
próximo next; la semana
  próxima next week
pues well

que that; than; es que it's
  just that
¿qué? what?; which?; ¿qué
  tal? how goes it?
quedar to have left; to
  remain; quedarse to stay;
  quedarse solo to be (remain) alone
quien who, whom
¿quién? who?; ¿de quién?
  whose?

rabiar to rage; hacer rabiar
  to infuriate
radical radical, root
razón (f.): tener razón
  to be right
realidad (f.) reality
recíproco reciprocal
reflexivo reflexive
regular regular
relativo relative
repente: de repente sud-
  denly
requerer (ie) to require
ridículo ridiculous
romántico romantic
romper to break

saber to know
salir to go out, to leave

se (ind. obj. pron. before
  lo, la, los, las) him, her,
  (form. sing. & pl.) you, them
secretaria (f.) secretary
sed (f.) thirst; tener sed to
  be thirsty
seguir (i, i) to go on, to
  follow, to continue
según according to
seguro sure, certain
semana (f.) week
sentido (m.) meaning
sentimental sentimental
sentir (ie, i) to feel, to
  be sorry
señor (m.) gentleman, man
señora (f.) lady, madam
ser to be
serio serious; en serio seri-
  ously
si if; but (often not tran-
  slated)
sí yes; ¿ah, sí? oh really?
siempre always; para siempre
  forever
siete seven
siguiente following
sin without
sincero sincere
sino but, but rather
situación (f.) situation
sobrevivir to outlive
solo alone
soy I am
son they, you are
sorprender to surprise
Sr. (señor) Mr.
su(s) (poss. adj.) his, her,
  (form. sing. & pl.) your,
  their
subjuntivo subjunctive
sucio dirty
sueño (m.): tener sueño to
  be sleepy
sugerir (ie, i) to suggest
sujeto (m.) subject
superlativo (m.) superlative
sustantivo (m.) noun

tal: con tal que provided
  that; ¿qué tal? how goes
  it?; ¿qué tal el café?
  how's the coffee?

también too, also
tampoco neither, not...
  either
tan so much
tanto so much; mientras
  tanto meanwhile
tarde (f.) afternoon
teatro (m.) theater
teléfono (m.) telephone
televisión (f.) television
temer to fear, to be afraid
temporal: expresión temporal
  (f.) expression of time
temprano early
tener to have; tener que to
  have to
tía (f.) aunt
tiempo (m.) tense, time;
  a tiempo on time
todavía still
todo(s) all, every
tomar to take
tonto perdido (m.) hopeless
  fool
traer to bring
tratar to treat
triste sad
tu (fam. sing.) your
tú (fam. sing.) you

Ud. (form. sing.) you
Uds. (form pl.) you
universidad (f.) university
un(o) a, an; unos some,
  several
uso (m.) use

valer to be worth; más vale
  que it is better that
vámonos let's go
¡vaya! well, well!
veces see vez
vender to sell
venir to come
ver to see
verbal verbal
verbo (m.) verb
verdad (f.) truth
vestido (m.) dress
vez (f.) time; muchas veces
  often, many times
víctima (f.) victim

vida (f.) life
viejo old; (m.) old man
vino (m.) wine
visitar to visit
vivir to live; ¡viva!
  long live!
volver (ue) to come back,
  to return
voz (f.) voice
vuelta: dar la vuelta al
  mundo to go around the
  world

y and
ya already; ya no no longer,
  not...anymore
yo (subj. pron.) I

This vocabulary is intended to be complete for all English words
in the Workbook.

a un(o)
able: to be able poder
about sobre, de; to talk
  about hablar de; to think
  about pensar en; what do
  you think about...? ¿qué
  piensa de...?
abrupt abrupto
abstract abstracto
academy academia (f.)
according to según
accuse acusar
adolescent adolescente (m.)
advise aconsejar
afraid: to be (very) afraid
  (of) tener (mucho) miedo
  (de); to be afraid (that)
  temer (que)
after después (de)(que); to
  ask after preguntar por
afternoon tarde (f.); it's
  three in the afternoon son
  las tres de la tarde; tomorrow afternoon mañana por
  la tarde
afterwards después
again otra vez
against contra
age edad (f.); when he is my
  age cuando tenga mi edad
ago hace; years ago hace años
agree estar de acuerdo (con)
all (of them) todo(s); all
  right bueno, está bien; (not)
  at all nada (en absoluto)
almost casi
alone solo
Alphonse Alfonso
already ya
alternative alternativa (f.)
always siempre
American norteamericano
amuse divertir (ie,i)
and y, (before i or hi) e
angry enojado; to get angry
  ponerse enojado
another otro
answer contestar
ant hormiga (f.)

anxiety angustia (f.)
any algún, alguno(s); any
  (at all) cualquier; not...
  any ningún, ninguno; I don't
  have any money no tengo dinero
anybody alguien; anybody (at
  all) cualquier(a); more than
  anybody (else) más que nadie;
  not...anybody nadie
anymore: not...anymore ya no,
  no...más
anyone alguien; anyone (at all)
  cualquier(a); more than anyone (else) más que nadie;
  not...anyone nadie
anything: not...anything nada
anyway de todos modos
anywhere cualquier parte;
  not...anywhere ninguna parte
apparently por lo visto
apple manzana (f.)
appreciate apreciar
April abril (m.)
are son; aren't they? ¿no?
argue discutir
around por; around here por
  aquí
arrive llegar
article artículo (m.)
artificial artificial
as tan, como, mientras; as
  adj. or adv.   as tan
  adj. or adv.   como; as
  noun   as tanto   noun
  como; as much as tanto
  como
ask (for) pedir (i,i); to
  ask (a question) preguntar;
  to ask after preguntar por
at a, en; (not) at all nada (en
  absoluto); at home en casa;
  at last por fin; at least por
  lo menos
attention: to pay attention to
  hacer caso a
attractive atractivo
August agosto (m.)
aunt tía (f.)

away: right away en
seguida

back: to get (come)
back volver (ue)
bad mal(o)
be ser, estar
beard barba (f.)
because porque; because
of por, a causa de
become hacerse
bed cama (f.) to go to
bed acostarse (ue); to
put to bed acostar
before antes (de que)
beg rogar (ue)
begin empezar (ie)
being: for the time being
por ahora
believe creer
belong pertenecer; it be-
longs to my sister es de
mi hermana; it belongs to
me es mío
besides además
best mejor
bet: I'll bet a que
better mejor; it's better
(that) más vale (que)
big grande; the biggest
el más grande; to be in
a big hurry tener mucha
prisa
bit: a (little) bit un poco
black negro
blissfully happy felicísimo
boat barco (m.)
body cuerpo (m.)
book libro (m.)
born: to be born nacer
boy muchacho (m.); little
boy niño (m.)
break romper
bring traer
brother hermano (m.)
businessman hombre de ne-
gocios (m.)
busy ocupado
but pero; sino
buy comprar
by (agent) por; (deadline)
para

calculation cálculo (m.)
call llamar
calm tranquilo; to calm
down calmarse
can poder
Canadian canadiense
capable capaz
car coche (m.); auto (m.)
case caso (m.); in case en
caso (de) que
cat gato (m.)
Catholic católico
cement cemento (m.)
child niño (m.) hijo (m.)
children niños (m. pl.);
hijos (m. pl.)
chocolate chocolate (m.)
city ciudad (f.)
class clase (f.)
clean limpio
close cerrar (ie)
coffee café (m.)
cold frío; to be cold
(weather) hacer frío;
to feel (very) cold
tener (mucho) frío
color color (m.)
come venir; to come back
volver (ue); to come in
entrar, pasar; come on!
¡anda!
common común
complain quejarse (de)
conquer vencer
contrary: on the contrary
al contrario
conversation conversación (f.)
convince convencer
cost costar (ue)
count contar (ue); count on
contar con
course: of course claro, por
supuesto, desde luego; of
course not! ¡claro que no!
cover cubrir (se)
crazy loco; to drive crazy
volver loco; to go crazy
volverse loco
criticize criticar
cruel cruel
cry llorar
cynical cínico

dance bailar
date (of calendar) fecha (f.)
daughter hija (f.)
day día (m.)
death muerte (f.)
deathbed lecho de muerte (m.)
December diciembre (m.)
decent decente
defend defender (ie)
delicious rico (with estar)
deny negar (ie)
desire deseo (m.)
die morir (ue, u)
dinner cena (f.); to have
  dinner cenar
dirty sucio
dish plato (m.)
do hacer
doctor (Dr.) doctor (Dr.);
  médico (m.)
door puerta (f.)
doubt duda (f.); dudar
doubtful dudoso
down: to calm down calmarse
dream (about) soñar (ue)
  (con); sueño (m.)
dress vestido (m.)
drink beber
drive: to drive crazy volver
  loco

each cada; each other (use
  reciprocal reflexive) uno
  al otro, unos a otros
early temprano
easily fácilmente
eat comer
egocentric egocéntrico
egoistic egoísta
eight ocho
eighteen dieciocho
eighth octavo
eighty ochenta
either: not...either tam-
  poco
elect nombrar
eleven once
emphatic enfático
English inglés
enjoy oneself pasarlo bien,
  divertirse (ie,i)
enormous enorme
enough: to be enough bastar

entire entero
eternal eterno
eternity eternidad (f.)
even though aunque
ever: not...ever nunca
every cada; every night
  todas las noches
everybody todo el mundo
everyone todo el mundo
everything todo
evident evidente
exaggerate exagerar
examine examinar
exceedingly rich riquísimo
excess exceso (m.)
explain explicar
extraordinarily stupid es-
  tupidísimo
extremely pretty lindísimo
eye ojo (m.)

fact hecho (m.); in spite of
  the fact that a pesar de que
fall caer; to fall in love
  (with) enamorarse (de)
family familia (f.)
famous famoso
fantastic fantástico
fast rápido, rápidamente
fat gordo
father padre (m.)
February febrero (m.)
feel sentirse, encontrarse;
  to feel (very) cold tener
  (mucho) frío; to feel like
  tener ganas de; to feel old
  estar viejo
fever fiebre (f.)
fewer menos
fifteen quince
fifth quinto
fifty cincuenta
find encontrar (ue); to find
  out enterarse de; I found
  out supe
fine: to be fine estar bien
finish acabar, terminar
first primero
five cinco
fix (up) arreglar
fool tonto (m.); hopeless
  fool tonto perdido
foolish tonto

for para, por; for being...
  por...; for the time being
  por ahora
force obligar
forever para siempre
forget olvidar
formula fórmula (f.)
forty cuarenta
four cuatro
fourteen catorce
fourth cuarto
Friday viernes (m.)
friend amigo (m.)
from de; where is he from?
  ¿de dónde es?
furious furioso; to make
  (somebody) furious poner
  furioso (a alguien)

general: in general por lo
  general
generous generoso
German alemán
get recibir; I got tuve; to
  get back volver; to get
  furious ponerse furioso; to
  get married casarse; to get
  (there) llegar (allí); to get
  up levantarse
girl muchacha (f.); girl friend
  novia (f.); little girl
  niña (f.)
give dar
glad: to be glad alegrarse (de)
go ir(se); to go for ir por;
  to go home ir(se) a casa; to
  go on continuar; seguir (i,i);
  to go out salir; to go to bed
  acostarse (ue); how goes it?
  ¿qué tal?
God: for God's sake! ¡por Dios!
good buen(o); good morning
  buenos días; good night
  buenas noches; to have a
  good time pasarlo bien, divertirse (ie,i)
grandfather abuelo (m.)
gray gris
green verde (with ser)
guitar guitarra (f.)

hair pelo (m.)

hairy peludo
half medio; half an hour
  media hora
ham jamón (m.)
hand mano (f.)
happy feliz
hate odiar
have tener; (auxiliary
  verb) haber; to have
  a good time divertirse
  (ie, i); to have left
  quedar; to have to tener
  que; not to have faltar;
  one has to hay que
he él
head cabeza (f.); I have a
  headache me duele la cabeza
health salud (f.)
hear oír
help ayudar
her (dir. obj. pron.) la; (ind.
  obj. pron.) le; (poss. adj.)
  su, ...de ella;(prep. pron.)
  ella
here aquí; here's hoping ojalá
hers (el) suyo, ...de ella
herself ella misma; (prep. pron.)
  sí misma; (reflexive pron.) se
hi hola
him (dir. obj. pron.) lo; (ind.
  obj. pron.) le; (prep. pron.)
  él
himself él mismo; (prep. pron.)
  se
his (poss. adj.) su, ...de él;
  (poss. pron.) (el) suyo,
  ...de él
history historia (f.)
hit pegar
home: at home en casa; to go
  home ir(se) a casa
hope esperar; here's hoping!
  ¡ojalá!
hopeless fool tonto perdido
hopelessly ugly feísimo
hospital hospital (m.)
hot caliente; to be (very)
  hot (weather) hacer (mucho)
  calor; to feel hot tener
  calor
hotel hotel (m.)
hormone hormona (f.)
hour hora (f.)
house casa (f.); at my house

en mi casa; in the house
en casa; to (Javier's) house
a casa de (Javier)
how? ¿cómo?; how are you? ¿cómo
 está(s)?; how generous he is!
 ¡qué generoso es!; how goes
 it? ¿qué tal?; how long have
 you been waiting? ¿cuánto
 tiempo hace que espera(s)?;
 how old is ...? ¿cuántos años
 tiene...?; know how saber
human humano
hundred cien(to)
hungry: to be (feel)(very) hungry
 tener (mucha) hambre
hurry: to be in a (big) hurry
 tener (mucha) prisa
husband marido (m.)
hypocritical hipócrita

I yo
idea idea (f.)
ideal ideal
idiot idiota (m. & f.)
if si; (in case) en caso (de) que
important importante
improve mejorar
in en; (after superlative) de
incredible: it seems incredible
 parece mentira
incredibly fat gordísimo
independent independiente
insect insecto (m.)
insist insistir
inspector inspector (m.)
intelligent inteligente
intend pensar (ie)   inf.
interest interés (m.); to take
 an interest in interesarse por
invite invitar
irregular irregular
irresponsible irresponsable
is es; isn't he? ¿no?
it (dir. obj. pron.) lo,la;
 (prep. pron.) ello

January enero (m.)
jealous celoso
July julio (m.)
June junio (m.)
just:it's just that es que

keep guardar; to keep quiet
 callarse
kill matar
kiss beso (m.)
know (to be acquainted with)
 conocer; to know (how)
 saber

last último; at last por fin;
 last night anoche; last year
 el año pasado
late tarde
laugh (at) reírse (de)
lawyer abogado (m.)
learn aprender
least menos; at least por lo
 menos; the least popular el
 menos popular
leave salir; dejar
lecherous old man viejo verde (m.)
left: to have left quedar
lemonade limonada (f.)
less menos
lesson lección (f.)
let dejar; let him do it! ¡qué
 lo haga él! let's eat comamos;
 let's go vámonos
letter carta (f.)
lie mentir (ie, i)
life vida (f.)
like como; like that así; to
 feel like tener ganas de;
 to like gustar; what is
 ...like? ¿cómo es...?
listen escuchar
literature literatura (f.)
little pequeño; a little (bit)
 un poco
live vivir; long live! ¡viva!
logical lógico
lonely solo
long largo; how long have you
 been waiting? ¿cuánto tiempo
 hace que espera?; long live!
 ¡viva!
look (at) mirar; how fat she
 looks! ¡qué gorda está!; to
 look for buscar
lose perder (ie); to get lost
 perderse
lot: a lot (of) mucho
love amor (m.); querer (ie); to
 fall in love enamorarse (de)

108

lucky: to be (very) lucky
   tener (mucha) suerte

made hecho; what is his house
   made of? ¿de qué es su casa?
make hacer; to make (somebody)
   angry enojar (a alguien); to
   make (somebody) furious poner
   furioso (a alguien); to make
   up hacer las paces
man hombre (m.); old man viejo
   (m.)
many muchos
March marzo (m.)
marry casar(se); to get married
   casarse (con)
masochistic masoquista
materialistic materialista
matter importar; it doesn't
   matter no importa; what's
   the matter (with you)?
   ¿qué (le) pasa?
May mayo (m.)
maybe quizás, a lo mejor
me (dir. or ind. obj. pron.)
   me; (prep. pron.) mí; it's
   me soy yo; with me conmigo
meal comida (f.)
mean querer decir
meanwhile mientras tanto
meat carne (f.)
meet (for the first time)
   conocer
member miembro (m.)
mention mencionar
Mexican mexicano
Mexico México
midnight medianoche (f.)
mine (el) mío
minute minuto (m.)
Miss señorita (Srta.)
modern moderno
moment momento (m.)
Monday lunes (m.)
money dinero (m.)
month mes (m.)
moon luna (f.)
more más
morning mañana; good morning buenos días; it's ten
   in the morning son las diez
   de la mañana; tomorrow morning mañana por la mañana

most más; the most famous el
   más famoso
mother madre (f.)
move mover (ue)
movies cine (m.)
Mr. señor (Sr.)
Mrs. señora (Sra.)
much mucho; as much as
   tanto como; so much
   tanto; very much mucho
music música (f.)
must deber
my mi(s)
myself yo mismo; (prep.
   pron.) mí mismo; (re-
   flexive pron.) me

name apellido (m.); nombre
   (m.); my name is... me
   llamo...; what is your name?
   ¿cómo se llama?
nap siesta (f.)
near cerca (de)
necessary necesario
need necesitar, hacer falta
neither...nor ni...ni
neurologist neurólogo
never nunca, jamás
new nuevo
next próximo; next week la
   semana próxima
night noche (f.); tomorrow
   night mañana por la noche
nine nueve
nineteen diecinueve
ninth noveno
ninety noventa
no no
nobody nadie
nonsense! ¡qué va!
noon mediodía (m.)
nor: neither...nor ni...ni
not no
note apunte (m.)
nothing nada
notice notar
November noviembre (m.)
now ahora; right now ahora
   mismo
nowadays hoy (en) día
number número (m.)

occur ocurrir
o´clock: it´s one o´clock
  es la una; it´s two o´clock
  son las dos
October octubre (m.)
of de
offer ofrecer (-zco)
often muchas veces
oh ah, ay
old viejo; lecherous old man
  viejo verde (m.); old man
  viejo (m.); how old is...?
  ¿cuántos años tiene...?;
  to be...years old tener...
  años
older mayor, más viejo
oldest: the oldest el mayor,
  el más viejo
on en; go on seguir (i,i),
  continuar
once una vez; once a day una
  vez al día; once in a while
  de vez en cuando
one un(o)
only sólo, solamente
open abrir
opportunistic oportunista
or o; (before o or ho) u
orange anaranjado
order mandar; in order to para
original original
other otro; each other uno al
  otro, unos a otros
ought deber
our (el) nuestro
ourselves nosotros mismos;
  (prep. pron.) nosotros mismos;
  (reflexive pron.) nos
out fuera; out of sheer spite
  por pura vileza; to go out
  salir
outlive sobrevivr
owe deber

parents padres (m. pl.)
park parque (m.)
part: the sad part lo triste
pass (by) pasar
past; it´s ten past two son
  las dos y diez
patience paciencia (f.)
patriotic patriótico
pay pagar; to pay attention

hacer caso a
peace paz (f.)
people gente (f.)
percent por ciento
permit permitir
person persona (f.)
perverse perverso
peso peso (m.)
pity: it´s a pity es (una)
  lástima, es una pena
place lugar (m.)
plan plan (m.); pensar (ie)
  inf.
play (an instrument) tocar
please por favor
poem poema (m.)
police policía (f.)
poor pobre; poor (little)
  thing pobrecito
popular popular
possessive posesivo (m.)
possible posible
prefer preferir (ie, i)
prepare preparar
president presidente (m.)
pretty lindo
prevent impedir (i, i)
priest cura (m.)
probably probablemente
problem problema (m.)
professor profesor (m.)
promise prometer
provided that con tal que
purpose: it serves no purpose
  at all no sirve para nada
put poner; to put on ponerse

quarter cuarto; it´s a quarter
  past one es la una y cuarto;
  itś a quarter to two son las
  dos menos cuarto
question pregunta (f.); it is
  a question of es cuestión de
quiet: to keep quiet callarse

radio radio (m. & f.)
raise levantar
read leer
ready listo (with estar)
realize darse cuenta (de)
really realmente; really?
  ¿sí?

reasonable razonable
red rojo
refuse negarse (ie) a; I
  refused no quise
remember recordar (ue);
  acordarse (ue) de
repeat repetir (i, i)
restaurant restaurante (m.)
return volver (ue)
rich rico; richer más rico;
  the richest el más rico
ridiculous ridículo
right: all right bueno, está
  bien; to be (very) right
  tener (mucha) razón; right?
  ¿verdad?; right away en
  seguida; right now ahora
  mismo
ruin estropear(se)
run correr; to run away
  huir

sad triste
sail: to set sail embarcarse
sake: for God´s sake! ¡por
  Dios!
salary sueldo (m.)
same mismo; the same book
  el mismo libro
Saturday sábado (m.)
say decir; to say hello
  saludar
scare dar miedo
second segundo
secretary secretaria (f.)
see ver
seem parecer
sell vender
send mandar, enviar
sentimental sentimental
September septiembre (m.)
servant criado (m.)
serve servir (i, i)
seven siete
seventeen diecisiete
seventh séptimo
seventy setenta
shake temblar (ie)
shall: use future tense
stay quedarse
still todavía
strange raro
stroll: to take a stroll

pasear(se)
strong fuerte
student estudiante (m. & f.)
study estudiar
stupid estúpido
succeed tener éxito
successful: to be (very) successful tener (mucho) éxito
such tal; such an idea tal
  idea; for such a rich man
  para un hombre tan rico
suggest sugerir (ie, i)
sun sol (m.)
Sunday domingo (m.)
super adj.: use absolute
  superlative
surprise sorprender

take llevar, tomar; to take
  a bath bañarse; to take a
  shower ducharse; to take
  a stroll pasear(se); to
  take an interest in in-
  teresarse por; to take for
  tomar por; to take off qui-
  tar(se)
talent talento (m.)
talk hablar
tavern taberna (f.)
teach enseñar
tell decir
ten diez
tenth décimo
than que
thank you, thanks gracias
that (dem. adj.) ese, esa
  (nearby), aquel, aquella
  (over there); (dem. pron.)
  ése, ésa (nearby), aquél,
  aquélla (over there);
  (neuter pron.) eso, aquello;
  (rel. pron.) que; so that
  para que; that way así;
  that´s all nada más; that´s
  why por eso
the el, la, los, las
their su, ...de ellos
theirs suyo, ...de ellos
them (dir. obj. pron.) los,
  las; (ind. obj. pron.) les;
  (prep. pron.) ellos
themselves ellos mismos; (prep.
  pron.) sí mismos; (reflexive

pron.) se
then entonces
there allí; there is, there
  are hay; there to be haber
these (dem. adj.) estos, estas;
  (dem. pron.) éstos, éstas
they ellos, ellas
thing cosa (f.); it's no small
  thing no es poca cosa; the
  good thing lo bueno
think pensar (ie), creer; to
  think about pensar en; what
  do you think of...? ¿qué
  piensa de...?
third tercer(o)
thirsty: to be (very) thirsty
  tener (mucha) sed
thirteen trece
thirty treinta; thirty-one
  treinta y un(o); it's one
  thirty es la una y media
this (dem. adj.) este, esta;
  (dem. pron.) éste, ésta;
  (neuter pron.) esto
those (dem. adj.) esos, esas
  (nearby); aquellos, aquellas
  (over there); (dem. pron.)
  ésos, ésas (nearby); aquéllos,
  aquéllas (over there)
though: as though como si; (even)
  though aunque
three tres
Thursday jueves (m.)
time hora (f.);tiempo (m.); vez
  (f.); a long time ago hace
  mucho tiempo; for the time
  being por ahora; to have a
  good time pasarlo bien, divertirse (ie, i); to have time
  tener tiempo; what time is it?
  ¿qué hora es?
tired cansado; to get tired
  cansarse
to a; a quarter to two las
  dos menos cuarto
today hoy
together juntos
tomorrow mañana; tomorrow
  night mañana por la noche
tonight esta noche (f.)
too también; demasiado; too
  much demasiado
touch tocar
travel viajar

treat tratar
tree árbol
tremble temblar (ie)
true: it's true es verdad (f.)
truth verdad (f.)
Tuesday martes (m.)
twelve doce
twenty veinte; twenty-one
  veintiún, veintiuno, veinte
  y uno
twice dos veces
two dos; the two of you (them)
  los dos
typical típico

ugly feo
unbelievable increíble
unbelievably pretty lindísimo
uncle tío (m.)
under debajo (de)
underneath it all en el fondo
understand comprender, entender (ie)
unfortunately por desgracia
United States Estados Unidos
  (m. pl.)
university universidad (f.)
unless a menos que, a no ser
  que
unripe verde (with estar)
until hasta
up: to make up hacer las paces
us (dir. & ind. obj. pron.) nos;
  (prep. pron.) nosotros

vacation vacaciones (f. pl.)
veritable verdadero
very muy; very much mucho
victim víctima (f.)
visit visitar

wait esperar
wake (up) despertar(se) (ie)
want querer (ie)
war guerra (f.)
warn advertir (ie, i)
wash lavar(se)
water agua (f.)
way: that way así
we nosotros
wear llevar

wedding boda (f.)
Wednesday miércoles (m.)
week semana (f.)
weep llorar
welcome: you're welcome de
  nada
well pues; bien
what lo que; he is what
  he is es como es
what? ¿qué?, ¿qué más
  da?; what about me?
  ¿y yo?; what is his
  house made of? ¿de
  qué es su casa?; what
  is...like? ¿cómo es...?;
  what time is it? ¿qué
  hora es?
when cuando
where donde; where? ¿dónde?;
  where is he from? ¿de
  dónde es?; where is he
  going? ¿adónde va?
which (rel. pron.) que
which ¿qué? ¿cuál?
while mientras (que)
white blanco
who (rel. pron.) que; who?
  ¿quién?
whom is it for? ¿para quién es?
whose cuyo; whose? ¿de quién?
why: that's why por eso; why?
  ¿por qué?
wife mujer (f.)
will: use the future tense
window ventana (f.)
wine vino (m.)
wise sabio
with con; with me conmigo;
  with you (fam. sing.) contigo; covered with cubierto
  de
without sin (que)
woman mujer (f.)
wonder preguntarse
word palabra (f.)
work trabajar
world mundo (m.)
worry preocuparse (por)
worst peor
worth: to be worth valer; to
  be worthless no valer (para)
  nada
write escribir
wrong: what's wrong (with me)?

¿qúe (me) pasa?; to be wrong
estar equivocado, no tener
razón

year año (m.); to be...years
  old tener...años
yellow amarillo
yes sí
yesterday ayer
yet todavía; not yet todavía no
you (dir. obj. pron.)(for.
  sing.) lo, (for. pl.) los,
  (fam. sing.) te; (ind. obj.
  pron.)(for. sing.) le, (for.
  pl.) les, (fam. sing.) te;
  (prep. pron.)(for. sing.) Ud.,
  (for. pl.) Uds.; (fam. sing.)
  ti; (subj. pron.)(for. sing.)
  Ud., (for. pl.) Uds., (fam.
  sing.) tú; with you (fam.
  sing.) contigo
young joven; younger menor,
  más joven; young man joven (m.)
your (for. sing.) su(s), ...de
  Ud.; (for. pl.) su(s), ...de
  Uds.; (fam. sing.) tu(s)
yours (for. sing.) (el) suyo,
  ...de Ud.; (for. pl.) (el)
  suyo, ...de Uds.; (fam. sing.)
  (el) tuyo
yourself Ud. mismo, Uds. mismos,
  tú mismo; (prep. pron.)(for.
  sing.) sí mismo, (for. pl.)
  sí mismos; (fam. sing.) ti
  mismo; (reflexive pron.) (for.
  sing. & pl.) se, (fam. sing.)
  te